	DATE DUE	
APR 23 2006		

Great Rabbit
and the
Long-tailed Wildcat

Retold by Andy Gregg
Illustrated by Cat Bowman Smith

ALBERT WHITMAN & COMPANY
Morton Grove, Illinois

Library of Congress Cataloging-in-Publication Data

Gregg, Andy.
   Great Rabbit and the long-tailed Wildcat /
Andy Gregg; illustrated by Cat Bowman Smith.
       p.   cm.
   Summary: Wildcat loses his beautiful bushy tail
after a confrontation with Great Rabbit.
      ISBN 0-8075-3047-6
      1. Algonquian Indians—Legends. [1. Algonquian
Indians—Legends. 2. Indians of North America—
Legends.] I. Smith, Cat Bowman, ill. II. Title.
E99.A35G74   1993
398.2—dc20   92-22950
[E]   CIP
                                                              AC

The text typeface is Stone Informal.
The illustration medium is Gouache.
Cover and typography design: Eileen Mueller Neill.

"Great Rabbit and The Long-tailed Wildcat" is loosely based on a story told by Passamaquoddy Indian Tomah Joseph to folklorist and author Charles Godfrey Leland (1824-1903).
It was first published as "Relating how the Rabbit became Wise by being Original, and of the Terrible Tricks which he by Magic played (on) Loup-Cervier, the Wicked Wild Cat," in *The Algonquian Legends of New England*, 1884.

To the people of the legend. C.B.S.

Long ago, when the world was young, the wildcat was a proud creature. He was proud of his sharp teeth and soft fur. He was proud of the tufts of hair on his pointed ears and of his handsome side whiskers. But he was most proud of his long, beautiful, bushy tail.

A long tail on a wildcat? A wildcat doesn't have a long tail. He lost it long ago, when the world was young.

One cold, snowy winter morning, Wildcat wanted to eat a rabbit. But he was too proud to eat just any small bunny. He decided to eat the chief of all rabbits, Great Rabbit himself.

Great Rabbit was the most powerful of all rabbits. He was big and smart and strong, and he was also magical. He lived in a wigwam in a thorny thicket in the middle of the forest, very far away from Wildcat. But Great Rabbit could hear Wildcat talking.

"I'm almost at his wigwam," Wildcat was saying as he ran through the woods. "Great Rabbit is sure to be my breakfast in a few minutes."

Great Rabbit heard that and thought, "If he's going to eat me, then I don't want to be home."

He leaped outside and jumped behind a tree. Then he sat down to listen, his ears waving in the wind.

Meanwhile, Wildcat arrived at Great Rabbit's home. He stuck his head inside and looked around, under the blankets, everywhere.

Great Rabbit wasn't there to be eaten!

"He can't do this to me!" Wildcat shouted. "I'll find him wherever he is, and I'll eat him! I bet my tail I can!"

Great Rabbit laughed when he heard that, and leaped off into the forest. At sundown, he trampled a little spot in the snow and waited for Wildcat.

Back at the wigwam, Wildcat started looking for Great Rabbit's tracks. He ran around in circles, each time going farther out, hoping to find some sign of Great Rabbit.

Wildcat came across Great Rabbit's tracks at noon. Then he ran until the moon was high in the sky and his bones ached.

Finally, he came to a clearing in the forest and saw a large wigwam standing tall in the moonlight.

Wildcat pulled aside the entrance flap and peeked inside. He saw soft blankets on the ground, and he smelled meat cooking over a hot fire.

A great medicine man, wrapped in a brightly colored blanket, sat beside the fire. He had long, narrow ears.

"Welcome," said the medicine man.

Wildcat was confused. The medicine man's ears looked very much like a rabbit's ears. Perhaps this was Great Rabbit playing one of his magic tricks.

"Hello," said Wildcat. "I can't help but notice that you have very long ears."

"I know," said the medicine man. "They are quite useful. I can pull them around my chin to keep it warm."

Wildcat was satisfied. He hoped he hadn't offended the powerful medicine man. Wildcat crept in, rolled onto his back, and allowed his furry tummy to be scratched.

Then he asked, "Have you seen any rabbits around here?"

"I see rabbits all the time," said the medicine man. "There are many of them running around in the bushes."

"I'm not looking for those," said Wildcat. "I want the ruler of rabbits, Great Rabbit himself. Have you seen him?"

"No, I can't say that I have," said the medicine man. "But you seem to be very tired. Why don't you rest for awhile?"

"I *am* very tired," said Wildcat. "I've been running since morning."

He crawled to a blanket and warmed himself by the fire.

"Are you hungry?" asked the medicine man.

"Yes, very," said Wildcat. "I haven't had anything to eat all day."

"I have a small rabbit roasting over the fire," said the medicine man. "Help yourself."

"Thanks," said Wildcat. "I don't mind if I do."

Although Wildcat really wanted to eat Great Rabbit, he was so tired and hungry that he thought even a small bunny would taste good.

He took the meat off the stick. The rabbit was very tasty. He put the bones in a neat pile on the ground. Then he yawned and arched his back and stretched. He wrapped his long, bushy tail around his nose and fell asleep.

Wildcat dreamed that he was chasing Great Rabbit. No matter how fast Wildcat ran, Great Rabbit was always far ahead, and he was laughing.

The next morning, Wildcat woke and yawned again, stretched again, and...

howled!

He leaped into the air. He was not inside a warm wigwam. He was alone in a small spot trampled in the frozen ground. He was stiff and cold and hungry.

"How can I be hungry?" he thought. "I ate a roast rabbit last night."

He looked at the place where he had put the rabbit bones the night before and found only a scrap of squishy squash.

"Gaack!" he screamed. "It wasn't rabbit I ate! It was a vegetable! Great Rabbit has tricked me!"

He wiped his tongue with the end of his tail.

Wildcat exclaimed, "I'll catch him if I have to run to the end of the rainbow!"

Wildcat ran in circles again, farther and farther out, until he found Great Rabbit's tracks. Then he ran until his legs were as weak as strings and he was so hungry that his stomach flapped like an empty bag inside his skinny ribs. He ran over the top of a mountain and down into the valley on the other side. He ran until the moon was high in the night sky.

Then he came to a cold, wet swamp. In the middle of it was a small hut of branches covered with brush. Wildcat waded through smelly, slimy green water until he arrived at the door of the hut.

"Maybe Great Rabbit is here," he said to himself.

But instead of Great Rabbit, a poor old woman was sitting beside the fire in the hut. She wore thin moccasins and a patched dress. A long braid stuck up on each side of her head.

"Welcome," said the old woman.

Wildcat thought, "I don't want to be fooled by Great Rabbit again."

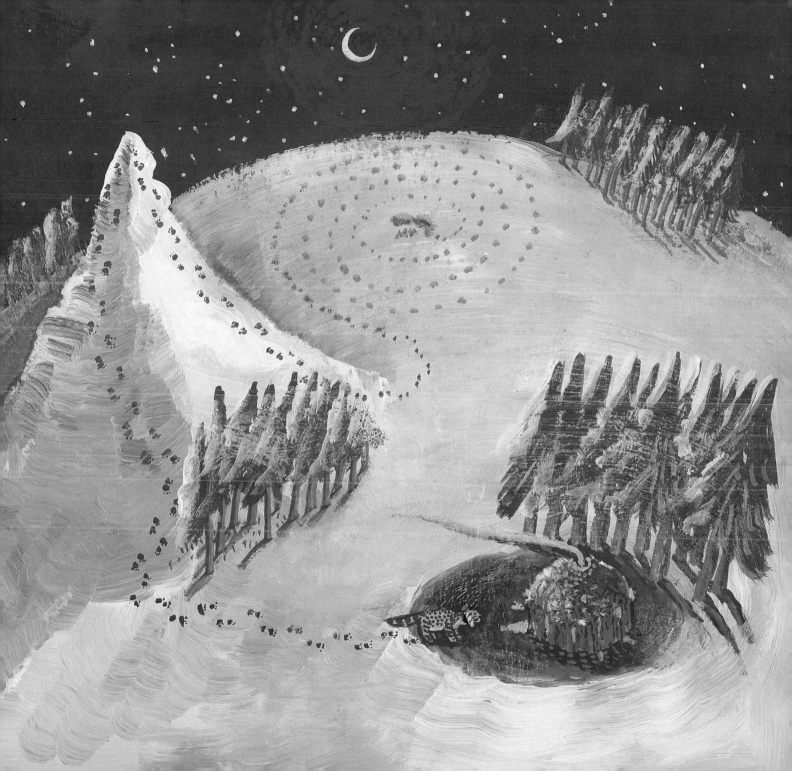

He nodded to the old woman and said, "Your braids look just like a rabbit's ears."

"Thank you," she said. "I've been told they are very attractive."

Wildcat was satisfied, and decided to pretend to be respectful, for the woman might have some food.

"You're such a lovely lady, I only wish that I could have brought you a present. Maybe a fat, juicy mouse. But I don't have even a mouse. For two days I've had nothing to eat but some squishy squash. Have you seen any rabbits around here?"

"There are many of them hopping around in the swamp," she said.

"I'm not looking for any little swamp hopper," said Wildcat. "I'm after the ruler of rabbits, Great Rabbit himself. Have you seen him?"

"No, I haven't," said the old woman. "But squash isn't fit food for a wildcat. You must be hungry. There's a rabbit cooking over the fire. Help yourself."

"Thank you," said Wildcat.

"My, you're polite for a wildcat," she said.

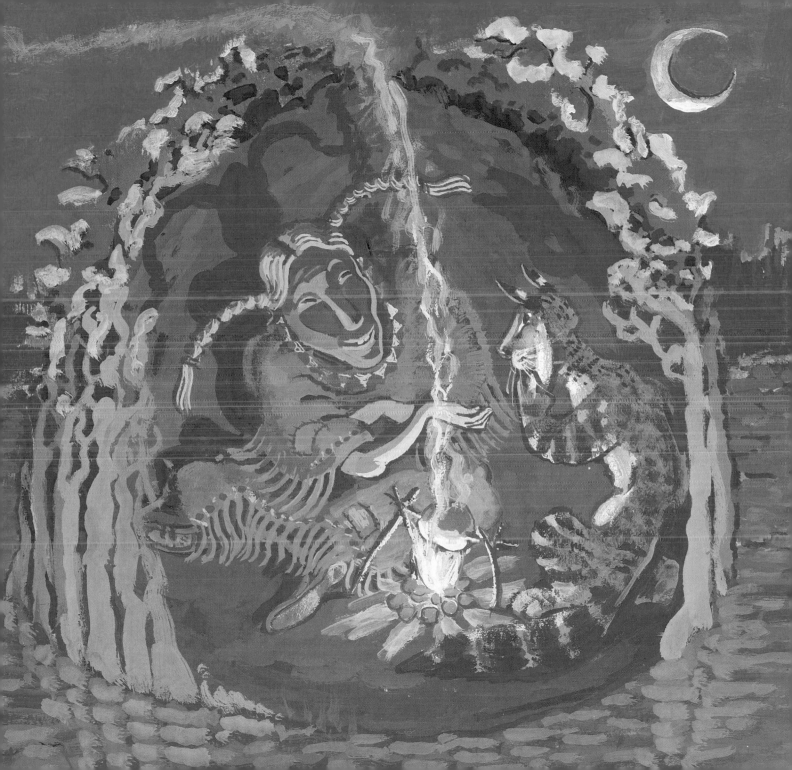

Wildcat ate the meat. It tasted very good. After he finished eating, he put the bones in a neat pile on the floor. Then he yawned and stretched, laid down beside the fire, and went to sleep.

This time when he dreamed of chasing Great Rabbit, Wildcat almost caught him.

In the morning, Wildcat woke and yawned again, stretched again, and...

yowled!

He was lying in a puddle of clammy water. There was no hut, no old woman, no cheerful fire.

He was cold and tired and wet and hungry.

"How can I be hungry?" he thought.

In front of him, where he had piled the rabbit bones, he saw there was only a blot of burned beans.

"Gaack!" he screeched. "I ate beans!"

He rinsed his mouth with greenish swamp scum.

"It was all Great Rabbit's magic again. I'll show him! I'll catch him if I have to run through the middle of next week!"

He ran around, going outward from the puddle,
until he found Great Rabbit's tracks. Then he followed
them, running until he was so thirsty that his tongue
dragged on the ground. He stepped on it fourteen
times, and three times he tripped over it.

But Wildcat was determined, and he ran on and on
into the night. When the moon was high, he finally
came to a large log hut in the middle of the forest.
Smoke floated up from a hole in the hut's mud roof.

He crawled through the bushes until he was at the
door of the hut. He thought, "I hope I've caught Great
Rabbit at last."

When he looked inside, he saw a great warrior. The warrior wore a large feather sticking up on each side of his head, and he had long feet covered with fur moccasins. He was busy sharpening a big tomahawk on a rock, but he noticed Wildcat.

"Welcome," said the great warrior.

"Somehow I knew you were going to say that," said Wildcat. "You know, those feathers in your hair look very much like the ears of a rabbit."

"So I've been told," said the warrior.

"And I couldn't help but notice that you have very long feet—like a rabbit's," said Wildcat.

"Of course I have long feet," said the warrior. "I have them for the same reason that a rabbit has. I can walk on top of the snow without sinking in up to my nose."

"You aren't a rabbit, are you?" asked Wildcat.

"Of course not," said the warrior. "Don't you like rabbits?"

"No!" Wildcat shouted. "For three days I've been chasing the ruler of rabbits, Great Rabbit himself! He has played his magic tricks on me. I have been sleeping in the snow and in the swamp. I have eaten nothing but squishy squash and burned beans."

Wildcat was so angry that he stood on his hind legs and waved his paws in the air. He danced up and down as he shouted:

"I hate Great Rabbit!
My fangs will stab him
when I grab him!
My jaws will grind him
when I find him!
I hate Great Rabbit!
And I will eat him
when I meet him!"

The great warrior stood up. His head almost touched the ceiling of the log hut. When he spoke, his voice was like thunder.

"YOU'VE FOUND HIM!"

The warrior's face suddenly became fierce and furry, with a mouth full of two large teeth. It was Great Rabbit himself!

The log hut disappeared, and Wildcat saw that he was really inside Great Rabbit's wigwam.

Great Rabbit waved the tomahawk. Wildcat squealed in fright as he ran around and around the flames.

Great Rabbit swung the tomahawk.

"You bet your tail," he shouted, "and you lost!"

The tomahawk cut off Wildcat's tail.

Wildcat put his paws where his tail should be, but it wasn't there.

"My tail!" he shrieked. Wildcat ran howling and screaming through the snowy forest.

Great Rabbit smiled, put up his feet before the fire, and settled down to eat a supper of crispy vegetables.

And Wildcat? Ever since that day, every wildcat has had only a short stump instead of a long, beautiful, bushy tail.